Do Not Fear.
Go Tell!

THE WORLD'S BIGGEST SECRETS

Adele Hebert

Scripture taken from KJ3 Literal Translation New Testament, Second Edition, Copyright © 2006.

Used by permission of the copyright holder, Mary V. Green.

KJ3 Literal Translation Bible verses are indicated by (KJ3).

Unless otherwise specified, all scriptures in this book are from KJ3 Literal Translation Bible.

Copyright © 2018 Adele Hebert

All rights reserved.

ISBN: -10: 1723364177

ISBN-13: -978-1723364174

WORDS OF LOVE
AND SELF CONTROL

My previous book, *Jesus Loves Women So Much,* was written to help young Ladies gain a strong self-esteem through the instructions in the Bible relating to Women.

Do Not Fear. Go Tell is God's Sex Education, words you've probably never heard.

Many parents do not read the Bible and therefore do not use these powerful guidelines to teach their children.

Schools do not teach these life principles of Love and Protection either.

<u>These studies will very likely be the</u>

<u>Most Important Teachings of Your Life!!!!</u>

Girls are taught from very young to be nice, to obey and to be submissive.

They are intelligent but their opinions are not valued. They are silenced so often that they learn Not to question what they are told.

Many young Ladies make mistakes early in life because of low self-esteem.

They Don't know how to make careful decisions because they Don't believe they <u>Deserve</u> to be treated with <u>Dignity</u> and <u>Respect</u>.

Women are easily deceived because they do not have this Valuable Foundation.

But even if you have messed up,

Always Remember that You are <u>LOVED</u>!

I believe Women can be strong but they need to learn to use their voice. This Bible study will help you gain a great self-esteem and avoid many tragedies in life.

SEEDS OF HOLINESS

DO YOU HAVE THE GUTS TO READ THIS?

This Valuable Information is almost NEVER talked about. I have NEVER heard it from a pulpit or from friends or family. I started reading my bible and found these unbelievable teachings. These are all GOD's Words, not my personal opinion.

These have to be the

WORLD'S BIGGEST SECRETS!

Please sit down as you read

GOD's

Most Life Changing Teachings.

GOD has a serious message about holiness, men's *Semen*, Women's periods and Who is unclean.

<u>Sex is to be holy</u>.

GOD has called us to be holy.

Men should live with their Wives in a Holy and Honorable way, not with lustful desires, like those who do not know GOD.

We must Control our own body in holiness and honor, and not be controlled by lust. (1Thess 4).

Most people think that men don't have

SELF CONTROL,

<u>BUT THEY DO!</u>

There are SO MANY laws given to the <u>men</u>, <u>by GOD</u>, but Women need to know them as well, to <u>DEFEND</u> themselves.

<u>Why is this stuff even in our Bibles???</u>

Because of tv, hollywood and the clothing industry, this young generation have bought into the sexual revolution.

Schools don't teach morals. Movies and books are filled with sex and violence. It is much more complicated than all that, but let's say we have neglected what GOD says, about modesty and love and respect.

GOD's words of advice to young Ladies are for their <u>PROTECTION</u>. GOD loves you and wants the <u>BEST</u> for you.

You don't have to even look for a husband. If you are meant to be married, the right man will come to you, and it will be a healthy relationship, not filled with anger and drama. Otherwise you could have a life of Sorrow.

GOD's Sex Education was not meant just for the Old Testament times.

You can say that we are more advanced now because we have Birth Control.

And realistically, who abstains nowadays?

And who wants twelve children?

However, nothing has changed. Women still get their periods. Men still have their *Semen*. Women still need time to heal after childbirth. Men still struggle with Self Control.

But where is the reverence for Women???

<u>SURPRISE -- Birth Control was invented so that men could have unlimited pleasure without the responsibility of an unwanted pregnancy.</u>

--- We are told Birth Control helps Women.

Many, many Women suffer their entire lives because they are deceived.

We are told that men mature later than Women, and should not get married too young.

--- We are told that men need lots of sex.

Women waste their childbearing years waiting for these immature guys, who make lots of promises.

Women also waste their childbearing years being on Birth Control, getting Ovarian Cancer, Ectopic Pregnancies, surgeries and having Abortions.

The whole burden is laid on Women to be responsible for family planning because they get pregnant.

Billions of dollars are spent each year on Women's Birth Control methods. You see commercials every day where the Woman is afraid that she may have forgotten her pills.

Nowadays, many products do not involve remembering pills, but they have their own side effects.

--- Men don't worry about anything.

There is no pressure put on men to use condoms, but Women are told repeatedly that men cannot be deprived… If you don't give him what he wants, he will go somewhere else to find it.

--- No one tells that to men.

<u>Fear</u> is also put on Women by doctors telling them that <u>They</u> Need to do something to prevent All these children.

--- No one puts fear on men.

Many Women still get pregnant using Birth Control.

If she does, it's all Her fault.

--- No one blames the man.

If a Woman does get pregnant, it's her body and she can have an Abortion if she wants.

--- We are told it's just a fetus anyway.

<u>GOD wants more for Women than that.</u>

<u>It's not about Birth Control.</u>

<u>It's about SELF CONTROL!</u>

Young ladies, Please I Beg You, look up the side effects of Birth Control. It is so serious, ranging from miscarriages to cancer to infertility to heart attacks, plus much more.

Women are pressured from parents, doctors, friends, and Especially boyfriends, to take Birth Control.

--- No one pressures the man.

I know that men <u>Don't. Want. To.</u> wear a condom, but they don't care if Women get sick and suffer and risk their lives! Many don't care if the Woman gets pregnant.

** Doctors don't tell you all the side effects because they want you to buy a monthly prescription. **

What's the big deal about virginity? Well, sorry Ladies, but guys really care about it, especially when they are getting married. It kind of assures them of your fidelity.

--- No one thinks about his virginity.

Living with a guy for five or ten years does not guarantee he will marry you.

Getting pregnant does not guarantee he will marry you.

Both will backfire.

Let the man prove that he values you.

Let him show you that he respects you and loves you.

SIMPLE

If you both want sex, he wears a condom.

SIMPLE

You Are So Precious.

Don't settle for a guy who doesn't think so.

But even if Women have sex using condoms for ten years, (and waste all their childbearing years) what does that prove? Will he marry her? If he hasn't yet…

Won't she Feel USED if she Wasted all those precious childbearing years?

Even if you are not a virgin, it doesn't mean that you Have to give your body anymore.

Only if you want to.

Only if he has a condom.

We are all weak, but don't be Foolish.

<u>You Are Very Precious</u>.

<u>If the man does not understand</u>

<u>the meaning of NO</u> --

<u>LET HIM GO!</u>

<u>** There's 50 Ways to Leave Your Lover **</u>

If your boyfriend even begins to Nag you for sex …

<u>Let Him GO!</u> <u>Never Look Back</u>!

He might buy you lots of meals and gifts. He might say he loves you today. He might appear to be everything you thought you wanted.

** If that's ALL he thinks about,

he doesn't love you. **

Warning – drinking and being alone with him could ruin your life. If he has his eye on your money or on other Women, …

<u>Let Him Go FAST!</u>

<u>If he really loved you,</u>

<u>he would not Nag you for sex.</u>

If he even begins to make you

<u>** PROVE your love for him **</u>

<u>** Let him Go IMMEDIATELY! **</u>

<u>You don't have to PROVE anything.</u>

<u>HE HAS TO!!</u>

<u>If he has Anger Problems, RUN…</u>

<u>*** Sleeping with him only Proves that</u>

<u>You Don't Love Yourself. ***</u>

He will say anything until he gets you. He will promise you the moon <u>until he gets you</u>.

Promises, promises. How many young Ladies have been <u>dumped</u> afterwards???

Once you sleep with him, often times <u>he</u> loses all respect. Once you sleep with him, <u>his</u> desires become insatiable.

Once you sleep with him, <u>you</u> are emotionally tied to him. Then it is so hard to leave.

<u>And all he wants is …. ONE THING ….</u>

<u>*** Sleeping with him often means you have a low self-esteem. ***</u>

<u>You can't win a man's love by sleeping with him.</u>

The right man will just be happy to be with you, and do things FOR you.

It's not about what pleasures you can offer him (<u>food and sex</u>). It's about what he can do FOR YOU.

He could build you a coffee table, or help you plant a garden or paint the shed, whatever you need help with.

You could learn to cook together, play cards, or cycle around the city and have a picnic.

You need to do things that you will do after you are married, not just go to the bar or parties.

He needs to ask you what YOU want to do.

He would plan to Marry you, Not live together. You need to spend many hours discussing beliefs, goals, and plans for the future.

If he even tries to talk you into

<u>Alternate Forms Of Sex</u> –

<u>GET AWAY FROM HIM NOW!!!!!</u>

You will NEVER FORGET those experiences.

You will live to <u>REGRET</u> them <u>Terribly</u>.

Seriously, would you want your Mother or Grandmother to be under that kind of pressure?

You will feel <u>SOOO DEGRADED</u>.

GOD wrote many things in the bible for Women's <u>Protection</u>.

__*** Your man MUST treat you in a Holy and Honorable way or it won't work! ***__

If he gets Angry, or puts you down or calls you names …

__RUN! And NEVER Go Back.__

__He is NOT Sorry!__

If he talks about your body (you're fat) or other Women's body parts (big boobs), those are Really Bad Signs.

__--- The BEST advice EVER ---__

__Even if you are half way down the aisle,__

__-- You Can Still Turn Around. --__

__It's better to be alone,__

__than to wish that you were.__

__** There's 50 Ways to Leave Your Lover **__

It's better Not to have children than to have children who disrespect you and disregard the Bible.

Foolish children cause their Mother's sorrow. Prov 10:1

Choose a man who Honors You, a man who will raise Godly children with you.

It is extremely important to say that sex, with love and respect in marriage, is a very beautiful and wonderful gift from GOD.

Far too often we read the tragedies, where Women are abused, lusted after and raped.

So many Women die at the hands of men, after being violently beaten and raped.

Far too often women keep their horrors to themselves, even married Christian Women.

There are many things Women Never Talk about until years later, some not even when the husband is dead.

The Ten Commandments were given for our benefit, to set us apart from the world, to teach us about being holy and unholy.

GOD was trying to purify His Chosen people, teaching them what was holy.

Right from Genesis we read about the seed of the Woman.

Then we hear that Women are unclean because of their periods!??

GOD speaking to the men:

Lev 15:1 And Jehovah spoke to Moses and to Aaron, saying,

Lev 15:2 Speak to the sons of Israel, and you shall say to them, *to* any man,

Menstrual blood is said to be unclean but, in fact, it is simply untouchable. (Lev 15).

* The Woman herself was NOT unclean. The blood and what she sat on was not to be touched, Naturally! *

Anyone who touched her or her bed or what

she sat on was unclean.

Lev 15:19 And if a woman's issue in her flesh is a flow of blood, she shall be in her impurity seven days; and whoever touches her shall be unclean until the evening.

Lev 15:20   And anything on which she lies in her impurity shall be unclean; and anything on which she sits shall be unclean.

Lev 15:21   And whoever touches her bed shall wash his clothes and bathe in water, and be unclean until the evening.

** It Does <u>NOT</u> Say That Women Are Unclean. **

<u>Who would want to touch her bed??</u>

<u>What kind of touch is GOD talking about??</u>

<u>Women have always been considered unclean …</u>

But <u>Only the ONES Who Touch Her</u> are <u>unclean</u>.

<u>The Bible says</u> –

<u>"whoever touches her shall be unclean"</u>

The Hebrew translates, "her separation," she shall be "put apart." *Gill's Commentary* says, "she shall be put apart <u>seven days</u>"; not out of the camp, nor out of the house, but might not go into the house of GOD."

Women were <u>Exempt</u> from going into the house of GOD for one week every month, through no fault of their own, but men could be <u>Forbidden</u> every day of the month, because of their own depravity. Huge Difference!

<u>Women were supposed to be left alone.</u> Anyone who touched them when they were on their menstrual cycle became unclean.

This is not a punishment for Women. It's a

<u>** Warning -- For Men To Respect Women</u>

<u>Do Not Touch! **</u>

Ironically, men call Women unclean, but the men are the ones who are unclean.

<u>The Bible says</u> –

<u>"whoever touches her shall be unclean"</u>

During her monthly cycle, the Woman's body is in a state of purification; it is cleansing.

Menstruation is not a taboo. It is actually sacred. <u>GOD Created Menstruation.</u>

A Woman is to be reverenced. She is to be protected and taken care of. Women were not to be touched or disturbed while sitting or lying down, during her "way of women." (Please read Gen 31).

"Misogyny is the hatred of, contempt for, or prejudice against women or girls. Misogyny can be manifested in numerous ways, including social exclusion, sex discrimination, hostility, and male privilege ideas, belittling of women, violence against women, and sexual objectification of women." – *Wikipedia*.

Are men afraid of blood?

Is that why men call Women names? Or…

Do They Hate Being Restricted From Sex?

Menstruation has always been Women's Protection, yet has been used to put Women down, as if they were dirty or diseased.

--- Women are Not Unclean.

This natural process was created by GOD.

Men must take care of Women, especially when they are weak.

Women who are bleeding are treated as if they have leprosy. Jesus corrected this horrible stigma.

The Woman who touched Him had been bleeding for 12 years. Jesus was not shocked when she touched Him.

Jesus did not see her as unclean. He healed her, called her Daughter and gave her a Blessing.

He accepted her with Love, not shame.

On the other hand, GOD has SO MUCH to say about man's *Semen*. It also was not created unclean. It, too, carries the Seed.

** *Semen* is sacred. **

Semen is not to be SPILLED or to be the product of selfish lust.

GOD is a jealous GOD and wants us to regard every aspect of our bodies as holy.

These scriptures are not about who is better. Women can lust also. GOD is teaching us about *Semen* and menstrual blood.

GOD speaking to the men:

Lev 15:1 And Jehovah spoke to Moses and to Aaron, saying,

Lev 15:2 Speak to the sons of Israel, and you shall say to them, *to* any man,

GOD wants us to love each other. Sex, with love and respect in marriage, is holy, * but every other occasion when *Semen* is emitted, is unclean! *

Tragically, there is so much sexual abuse and Rape, even in marriage, the main culprit being the mis-use of scripture, like this verse "Do not deprive one another..." (1 Cor 7:5) or "your body is not your own."

DO MEN HAVE SUCH LITTLE SELF CONTROL?

Must men commit adultery if they don't get <u>Frequent Sex</u>??

Men have <u>HUGE Expectations</u> and <u>Entitlements</u> regarding sex.

They use <u>VIOLENCE and RAGING ANGER</u> until they get what they want.

"Do not deprive"…

Sadly, is used as a weapon!

Then there's the problem of "<u>submit</u>."

Even the marriage vows of 'love, honor and <u>obey</u>' have done so much harm, <u>keeping Women in sexual bondage.</u>

THE *M...* WORD

*** GOD seriously warns men about *Masturbation*! ***

Lev 15:16 "And if any man's *Semen* goes out from him, then he shall bathe all his flesh in water, and be unclean until the evening.

Lev 15:17 And every garment, and every skin on which the *Semen* is, shall be washed with water, and be unclean until the evening."

*** *Semen* Emitted By *Masturbation* Is Unclean! ***

"By the *Semen*, not only were the persons themselves defiled, but also every article of clothing or leather upon which any of the *Semen* fell." – *Keil and Delitzsch.*

It was for the purpose of purification, that men had to bathe, and that their clothing needed to be washed, because of their <u>lust and *Masturbation.*</u>

And because it was unclean, the men had to wash their own dirty laundry...

<u>Guard your minds!</u>

<u>Guard your *Semen*!</u>

Before GOD would be revealed on Mount Sinai, Moses was told to <u>consecrate</u> the people.

They had to <u>wash their garments</u> and <u>Abstain</u> from <u>sex for three days</u>.

Exo 19:14, 15 "And Moses went from the mountain to the people. And he sanctified the people, and they washed their clothes."

"And he said to the people, Be ready for the third day. <u>Do not approach a woman.</u>"

Their clothing needed to be washed, but three days were needed for the purifying of their minds from all sin and lust.

It was not because Women were unclean that men had to stay away from them. It was their minds that had to be purified.

"Wandering thoughts must be gathered in, impure affections abandoned, disquieting passions suppressed, before GOD will come to meet us." – *Matthew Henry*.

When GOD told the people not to have sex for three days in advance, it was to train the people not to dwell on lust. Our minds need to be focused Only on GOD, if we are to meet GOD.

GOD wants us to be a holy people. Sex is to be holy. We must keep a reverence for each other, for ourselves, and foremost for GOD. "Be holy as I am holy."

GOD clearly warns men to Abstain from unnatural sexual practices, if they want to be consecrated and in relationship with GOD.

GOD does not want men to SPILL their *Semen!*

Remember Onan? GOD Killed him for Spilling his *Semen* on the ground. Gen 38:9

Sex is to be holy –

No One Using each other!

God is very specific about the words *Seed* or *Semen*. Onan was deliberately depriving the Widow of a child.

---- Even Worse ----

** this was the *Seed in the line of Christ!!!!*

That is why God killed Onan. He was supposed to be in the genealogy of Christ but he SPILLED *The Seed on the ground*.

God saw this as the unforgiveable sin, so He killed Onan. Tamar was forced to be with Judah and they became the ancestors of Jesus.

There are many laws written and directed at the <u>men</u> regarding their *Semen*. Why did God need to instruct <u>men</u> so much??

Deu 23:10 "If there is among you *any* man who is not clean because of a discharge at night, then he shall go to the outside of the camp; he shall not come in to the middle of the camp."

<u>Even accidental emission of *Semen*</u>

<u>(Wet Dreams) make a man unclean!</u>

Being outside the camp was no small consequence; there was no food or water or shelter or bed there. No one could bring you anything or talk to you or touch you.

"By this trouble and reproach, which <u>even involuntary pollutions</u> exposed men to, men were <u>taught to keep up a very great dread of all fleshly lusts</u>." – *Matthew Henry*.

<u>** Stern Warning NOT To Look At</u>

<u>PORNOGRAPHY! **</u>

Also, Lev 22:4 _Semen is in the same sentence as touching a corpse!_ GOD wants our minds, our bodies and our clothing to be completely clean, <u>fearfully pure and holy.</u>

<u>Abstinence prepares us for holiness.</u> These decrees have been set out for us <u>by GOD</u> to purify us, to help make us a <u>holy nation, a Royal Priesthood.</u>

David and his army of men were hungry and went to the priest, asking for five loaves. Men were specifically told to <u>Abstain from sex during war</u>. (1Sa 21:4) "And the priest answered David and said, *There* is no common bread under my hand, but only holy bread, if the young men have only been <u>kept from a woman</u>."

"And David answered the priest and said to him, Surely, a woman *has been* kept from us as yesterday and the third *day*, since I came out, and the vessels of the young men are holy." (1Sa 21:5)

Before we partake of the holy bread, communion on the Sabbath, GOD wants us to be pure inside and out, <u>not having any thought of lust</u> for at least <u>three days prior.</u>

"David pleads that he and those that were with him, might lawfully eat of the hallowed bread, for they were not only able to answer his terms of keeping from women for <u>three days past,</u> but the vessels, the <u>bodies and clothing of the young men</u>, were also clean and holy, being possessed in sanctification and honour at all times." – *Matthew Henry.*

<u>* We need SELF CONTROL to be holy. *</u>

Before GOD came down to meet the people, the men had to Abstain from sex for three days.

Before David's men received holy bread, they had to Abstain from sex for three days. <u>It is lust that GOD hates.</u>

There are fundamental differences between menstrual blood and *Semen*:

<u>NOTE:</u> <u>Women's periods are involuntary</u>; they have no choice; Women have to have them; all Women have them; Women have no control over when they come or how long they last. <u>* *Semen* is mostly voluntary. *</u>

NOTE: Women do not get their periods as a result of lust. * *Semen*, on the other hand, is closely connected to lust. * Men have choices over their *seminal* emissions.

Wet dreams are not always in man's control, but they do correspond to what a man dwells on during the day.

If he fills his mind with PORNOGRAPHY,

chances are he will have wet dreams.

But even when it is 'innocent,' nevertheless GOD says he is unclean because *Semen* was SPILLED.

GOD wants even our dreams to be pure.

NOTE: Women were never sent out of the camp during their periods. * Men were always sent out of the camp if *Semen* was SPILLED. *

So where does Birth Control fit in?

Isn't that the same as *Spilling* our *Seed*?

What about using condoms?

You might say this is just the Old Testament but men are continuously warned not to lust in the New Testament also!

Besides, <u>Jesus didn't die from Abstaining. John the Baptist didn't die from Abstaining.</u>

In Mat 1:25, Joseph did not know Mary until she had her son Jesus. <u>Joseph didn't die from Abstaining!</u>

There is much preaching about Joseph being a good husband and father, but I have Never heard anything about <u>his Abstinence.</u>

Paul used to beat his body into submission. Paul had fear!

There are MANY verses referring to lust and SELF CONTROL in the New Testament. We have to answer for our actions.

GOD still sees behind closed doors and will judge us accordingly. We need to flee from lust! Be holy.

** *Seed* is sacred.**

GOD wants us to Abstain from sex Before Marriage, ... BUT ...

** Abstinence Is Also Necessary

<u>D U R I N G</u>

<u>Marriage. **</u>

NOTHING can prepare you for the amount of RAPE you may experience in marriage, unless you have a GOD fearing husband or unless he has some respect for your pain.

The Worst Raging BEAST comes out when he can't have sex, when there is no one around to Protect you.

It is Shocking, Unspeakable and

PAINFUL!!!

I am not making this up. Believe me, I guarantee that some of your friends will tell you in time.

All Women need their Mother or Sister to stay with them after a child is born ... to help with baby, but also ... to Protect them from RAPE.

When a Woman has her period, the husband is not to even touch her bed!

For seven days!

After a Mother has a baby, she needs to be left alone!

When a Woman is sick, she needs to be left alone!

When a Woman has surgery, she needs to be left alone!

When a Woman is SLEEPING, she needs to be left alone!

After a Mother gives birth, she needs WEEKS, left alone, to recuperate!

How many men HARASS and TORMENT a new Mother Before her body is Healed?? … claiming their right?

How many Mothers wish they could escape?? … but there is no place to go!

How many Mothers have to FIGHT OFF their husbands after childbirth?!?!

Some men have even been caught while the Mother is still in the hospital!!!

I went to visit a new Mother after she was home <u>only a few hours</u>, (a relative!), and there was a condom in the toilet!! I wanted to cry with her.

<u>--- Marriage is NOT a license for Unlimited Sex! ---</u>

<u>That is NOT love! That is RAPE!!!</u>

<u>PAINFUL RAPE!!!!!</u>

<u>*** I CAN NOT Repeat what many Women have told me – UNSPEAKABLE, degrading acts which men DEMAND, when Women are unable to have sex. PURE EVIL.</u>

<u>Men need to stop Hunting and Badgering and RAPING Women! A Woman must feel safe in her own bed! A Woman must feel safe to sit on her own chair!</u>

<u>** Men will have to answer to GOD!!! **</u>

You might say that it is not realistic for today's Women to stay home, just so that no one touches her.

How could Women not work for one week out of every month? We need doctors, lawyers, nurses, cooks, waitresses, banks, offices.

Read the verses again, "whoever <u>touches her</u> AND what she <u>sits on</u> AND <u>her bed</u>… is unclean." The verses all begin with "<u>And</u>," so they are all connected.

These verses are addressing <u>Only One person – Someone in the home!!</u>

Who else would touch her bed?

** Touching a Woman at work is <u>NOT</u> the same as a man touching her at home. **

At work there is <u>No</u> sex initiated or implied.

* These verses have <u>NO</u> restriction for Women working. *

These verses are <u>NOT</u> telling us that Women are unclean.

*** GOD Is Telling <u>Men</u> To

<u>Leave Women Alone!!</u> ***

* GOD Is Speaking To Husbands –

Do Not Touch!! *

What kind of touch is GOD talking about??

Who would want to touch her bed??

Co-workers would not want to touch her bed. People at the store would not want to touch her bed. Friends and bosses and neighbors would not want to touch her bed.

Who wants to touch her? AND

Who wants to touch her bed?

-- Only A Selfish Man Demanding Sex!!! --

These Verses Are Warnings Meant

Only For Husbands!!!

GOD is very clear – men must

--- NOT SPILL their *Seed*! ---

God <u>Killed</u> Onan for that.

God does not kill Women for menstruating.

Sexuality is directly linked to holiness.

Jesus strictly warned men

Not to even Look at a Woman with lust.

Thank GOD for these definite guidelines from the Word of GOD.

* These are Severe Warnings *

For Men To Respect Women.

* Do Not Touch! *

* These are Severe Warnings *

For Men

- Not To Lust,

- Not to RAPE

- Not to Spill Their *Seed!*

- Not to Masturbate

The road to holiness is paved with much

SELF CONTROL.

Jesus had to straighten out men's thinking about Who is unclean.

Mat 15:18 But the things which come out of the mouth come forth from the heart, and these defile the man.

Mat 15:19 For out of the heart come forth reasonings, evil *things*, murders, adulteries, fornications, thefts, lies, blasphemies.

I have never read anything honorable about Lev 12. Commentaries are extremely negative and downright cruel. Some say that boys were unclean because they participated in their mother's pollution, using words like shame, corruption and degradation.

What is GOD's loving interpretation?

What is GOD telling the sons of Israel???
Lev 12:2

Lev 12:2 Speak to the sons of Israel, saying, If a woman has conceived seed, and has borne a male, then she shall be unclean seven days; as on the days of her menstrual impurity she shall be unclean.

Lev 12:3   And on the eighth day the flesh of his foreskin shall be circumcised.

Lev 12:4   And she shall remain in the blood of her cleansing thirty three days; she shall not touch any holy thing, and she shall not go into the sanctuary, until the days of her cleansing are fulfilled.

Lev 12:5   And if she bears a female, then she shall be unclean two weeks, as in her menstruation; and she shall continue in the blood of her cleansing sixty six days.

Why did GOD write these laws -- for men?

At first I resented these verses. It does not seem fair, but remember, for Women, unclean does not mean dirty or diseased; it simply means 'untouchable.'

She is to be Left Alone, that's all. She is Ritually Unclean, purifying and cleansing.

Although Women were Exempt from going into the sanctuary, men were Forbidden to go if they *Masturbated.*

Now, as for the days of purification, these are exactly double for baby Girls. This does not mean she is being punished because she is twice as unclean as men.

* <u>She is to be Protected Twice as much!</u>

<u>This law is from GOD</u> -- <u>for men.</u> *

A Woman's body is a living sanctuary, for a New Life, and needs to be <u>Set Apart</u>. Menstruation, pregnancy and child birth were considered an 'infirmity,' but Women are <u>Not Sick</u>.

Women just have to be separated for a while, in order to heal.

The blood is a <u>Natural Cleansing</u>,

<u>Created by GOD</u>.

It is <u>Not Bad</u>, <u>Not Corrupted</u>, <u>Not Shameful</u>.

Women generally take care of each other when they are pregnant and giving birth.

Mary went quickly to help Elizabeth. Ruth had Naomi and Rahab and other Women by her side.

To be Set Apart means it is a <u>Special season for the Women, to appreciate the Blessings of GOD</u>, when Women don't have to cater to a man, when they can rest and restore their bodies.

Today's Women do not know what a privilege it is to be able to rest, to heal, and to bond with their new baby.

Many are sent home within a day. Many have a house full of people waiting. They are weak, but are forced to cook and clean and look after baby, with hardly any sleep and a host of medical issues, like <u>Pain</u>, and not being able to sit down.

Then there's the nagging husband. Some men are really jealous of a new baby, especially if it is a Girl.

<u>--- Perhaps being Set Apart is not so unfair after all…</u>

During pregnancy and childbirth, Women give their bodies as a living sacrifice, in co-operation with GOD the Creator.

This should be a special opportunity for bonding and for reflecting on the precious privilege it is to be born a Woman, and especially to have a Valuable Daughter.

What is GOD telling the <u>sons of Israel???</u>
Lev 12:2

<u>Women and Girls Need Extra Protection.</u> First of all, they need to be <u>Valued Enough to Live.</u> Before they are even Born, baby Girls are <u>Aborted by the Millions.</u>

Many hundreds of thousands of baby Girls are <u>Killed at Birth</u>, by leaving them in the hot sun on the side of the road or thrown in trash cans.

When they are young, Girls are often <u>Not Safe</u> in their own homes. They are easy prey for those who want to <u>Sexually Violate</u> them.

Now, More Than Ever, Girls are being <u>Deceived and Drugged</u>, then <u>Sold for Sex Trafficking</u>. (Young boys get raped also. It is all So Evil.)

Thousands of young Girls are <u>Burned with Acid</u> because they will not agree to get married to old men, or because they <u>Want to Go To School.</u>

Millions of Girls, every year, are <u>Mutilated</u> so they will <u>Never Enjoy Sex.</u> Many are so <u>Butchered</u> that they are not able to <u>Hold Their Urine.</u> They have Never-Ending <u>Pain and Surgeries.</u>

Women and Girls, worldwide, are the Main Targets of being <u>Stalked, Raped, Beaten, Killed</u>…

For Centuries, <u>Foot Binding</u> was common practise. Now there is <u>Breast Ironing</u>, to deter unwanted male attention, pregnancy and rape!

Lots of Pressure is put on Women for Appearance, including <u>Weight Loss Surgeries,</u> <u>Breast Implants,</u> <u>Piercings</u> and <u>Plastic Surgeries</u>. Where will it end?

Today, <u>Honor Killings</u>, <u>Forced Child Marriages</u>, <u>Force Feeding</u> if young Girls appear too thin for marriage.

Contraception is either forced or not allowed. Mob Violence if Women are Single and Independent, Prostitution, Abuse of Widows, Pornography, Forced Sterilization.

Alienation from Grandchildren, Abandonment of Seniors. Stoning for Getting Raped, Forced Suicide for Seniors, Cyberbullying.

Elder Abuse financial and physical, Co-signing of Property and Wills, Domestic Violence, Child Custody taken from the Mother… there is NO END to the Violence done to Girls and Woman.

These Atrocities are all Forced upon Women and Girls.

--- No Punishment For Men.---

Girls Need So Much Extra Protection, Right from Birth.

For some baby Girls, this is the Only time in their lives when they are safe, in the arms of their Mother.

GOD made many laws for men

to Teach them that <u>Women and Girls</u>

<u>NEED Extra Protection.</u>

Women are living sanctuaries, co-creating, birthing, nurturing, shedding blood naturally, set apart, sacrificing their lives... for a New Life… something <u>Women are Designed</u> to do.

Women and Girls are the <u>Future Generation</u>. They need to be taken care of.

Women need time to heal.

They need to be cherished, not abused.

What is GOD telling the <u>sons of Israel???</u>
Lev 12:2

<u>Men are Designed to follow GOD's laws</u> for their family, to Ensure that Mothers and baby Girls are Cherished, Protected, Bonded, Healthy, Safe and Stable.

GOD <u>EXPECTS</u> men to look after and <u>PROTECT</u> and <u>HONOR their Females</u>.

Baby Girls really need extra care from their Mothers, before they enter a very unloving world.

JESUS LOVES WOMEN SO MUCH!!!

Woman was the last wonderful work of GOD's creation, on the sixth day. At the end of every other day, GOD said it was "good." But on the last day, after creating the Woman, GOD said it was "very good."

OUR GOSPELS – MEMOIRS OF WOMEN

The Royal Commission for Women to use their voice to "GO and TELL" was not meant to happen only once, like an errand, on Resurrection morning. Our Gospels have survived precisely because <u>Women told and retold and retold</u> their experiences!

It is no accident that Jesus appeared to Women Only. It was foretold in three verses (Ps 68:11, Is 40:9, Joel 2:28) that Women were to be <u>Heralds, Lady Evangelists, Preachers of the Resurrection, Gospel</u>, but

<u>Tragically, in most Bibles the "Women" words have been removed!!</u>

Beginning with the four outstanding Women in the genealogy of Jesus and Mary's Conception, right through to Peter running to the empty tomb and the male disciples not believing the Women who saw the Lord after He had Risen, you will see the faithfulness and loyalty of the Women.

Our Gospels are overflowing with information that <u>Only Women</u> would have known about or would have dared to repeat.

Young Mary had the most amazing faith, but she could not share her treasured moments until after Jesus rose from the grave.

Can you imagine trying to keep that <u>colossal secret</u>???

She revealed about the angel Gabriel appearing to her, telling her not to be afraid, and how she consented to the plan of Salvation, to give birth to the "Son of GOD."

Mary went quickly to see her cousin Elizabeth who shouted, "And *she* cried out with a loud voice and said, Blessed *are* you among women and blessed *is* the fruit of your womb!" (Luke 1:42)

How comforted Mary would have been when Elizabeth exclaimed loudly that she was carrying her "Lord."

We are so fortunate to have Mary's Magnificat.

When Elizabeth's son was born, she defied tradition and stated emphatically what his name would be, standing up to all her neighbors and relatives.

How wonderful that Mary gave us so many details like "no place for them in the inn," where she had her baby, when the shepherds and the wise men came, and how they had to escape to Egypt at night.

<u>Our Christian faith Begins with Mary.</u>

We rely on Mary's knowledge of what happened from Jesus' Conception, to the cross and even after the Resurrection. She traveled with Jesus for three years and would have recollected many fine points of His ministry.

Mary, along with other Women, also received the Holy Spirit on Pentecost.

We would never have the privilege of knowing about the birth of Jesus, the infancy narratives or Elizabeth's great faith and boldness, without Mary's testimonies.

Mary's personal experience of what happened at the cross is So Valuable.

Mary's memories are a treasure, indeed!

Our Gospels are comprised mostly of the memoirs of the Women in Jesus' life, especially His Mother Mary and Mary Magdalene. These scriptures have prevailed because Women used their voice.

*** Women were the

Only Ones There At The

Conception and The Resurrection. ***

It was <u>Mary</u> who told us about the Angel. She was Chosen to bear Jesus, the "Son of GOD."

It was <u>Mary Magdalene and the Women</u> who gave their priceless observations about the Resurrection.

After Jesus appeared <u>Only to the Women</u>, they told the disciples and Peter that they must go over "<u>there</u>" to <u>Galilee</u> to see the Risen Lord.

*** Our Christian faith is based completely on the words of Women. ***

For decades, poor Mary had to stay silent about her Son, "And Mary kept all these words, meditating in her heart." (Luke 2:19)

Now, Mary Magdalene shattered the silence

and burst forth with the Greatest News Ever

Jesus rose from the grave!!!!

It is clearly the Women after the Resurrection who deserve the credit for giving us our Gospels.

Suddenly, these Women became well-known and respected for their great wealth of information.

Women's recollections were immediately sought after. They remembered Jesus' miracles and His teachings and many details of events.

It was the Women who passed on their personal experiences and their knowledge.

So much of what Jesus did or said affected them and their children.

Jesus gave Women the honor of being reliable witnesses and they were valued for sharing their memories.

Without these Chosen Women, we would have No Gospels.

----

* Many of the Gospel records were totally embarrassing for the men because of their lack of faith or because of their abusive behavior and attitudes towards Women and children. *

You can be sure that men did not brag about being made mute.

What about when Jesus wrote in the sand? What about the Woman with blood?

We definitely would not know about all the baby boys who were killed.

Women would have told about the conversation with the Samaritan Woman (five husbands and living with a man) who evangelized her whole city?

We would not know about the warnings for men Not to Lust after Women, had the Women not spread those words.

Naturally, men would have wanted to forget all the names Jesus called them and how often they were silenced and rebuked.

How about all the occasions when the men mocked Jesus?

Men would have never announced that Women can leave their husbands.

> How would we know that Jesus had to defend the Mothers who brought their children?

> Men would not have told us they devoured the houses of Widows?

It was plain insulting to be told that prostitutes will enter first and that if men want to be great they must serve everyone else.

It is not likely that men would have talked about the yeast of a Woman or about the Virgins with oil, or about the young Girl brought back to life.

Surely, it was Women who recalled when they were weeping and begging and praising GOD.

I wonder who told about the old Widow Anna. She was the first to "GO and TELL" about the Redeemer.

Only Women would have relayed all the problems Mary of Bethany had by sitting at His feet. Mary also anointed Jesus, while being criticized by angry men.

Women would have cherished how Jesus took their children in His arms.

Only the bold Gentile Woman would have appreciated how Jesus healed her Daughter.

Only Pilate's Wife would have given us the message about her dream.

Women alone disclosed all these events, and they most likely got in trouble for telling.

Most of the accounts in the Gospels were too humiliating for the men to want to share, like when the two brothers got their Mother to ask if they could sit next to Him in the kingdom.

Those in the synagogue ruler's house had no faith and ridiculed Jesus.

Men would have been ashamed to admit that rich men will hardly enter the kingdom.

> The disciples scolded the Mothers who brought children to Jesus.

How about when all the men in the synagogue tried to throw Jesus over the cliff?

Other records would have been of no interest to the men.

The men would not have boasted how great it was for a barren Woman to have a child in her old age.

The bent Woman was healed on the Sabbath. The men were so angry.

How about the Widow with two coins?

> Only Women would have marveled how Jesus cared for pregnant and nursing Mothers.

You can almost see the Women smiling when Jesus said they won't be married in heaven.

During Jesus' ministry, there is not much that Peter could be proud of. Jesus called Peter "Satan" in three Gospels.

We read that Peter tested Jesus so that he could also walk on water, but he began to sink when he saw the boisterous wind.

Peter declared that he would die for Jesus, but then he could not stay awake for one hour. Peter arrogantly refused to let Jesus wash his feet, telling Him to wash his hands and his head, also.

In the garden, Peter impulsively cut off a soldier's ear, which Jesus had to heal.

While Jesus was being whipped, Peter denied knowing the Lord to the servant-Girl.

And Mary Magdalene got the bad reputation?

Women would never forget how Jesus consoled them when they were wailing.

Jesus wept with Martha and Mary.

We would know nothing about the Women who followed Jesus if they hadn't reminded others later. They are the ones who supported those men for three years, with their own resources.

We would not know about the children praising in the temple, if the Mothers had not recalled that special day.

Now we know that we are Daughters.

GOD sees the joy of a Woman who finds her lost coin.

Now we know that children have angels who continuously look on the face of GOD.

Only Women would have related to each other not to worry so much and that few things are needed.

Jesus even knows when Women are distracted and anxious and troubled about many things. He sees that Women are pressured and that too much is expected of them.

Jesus appreciated the child who offered his bread and fish to feed the hungry.

If Women would not have hung onto and persisted about the Woman caught in adultery, it would have been lost Forever!

Women would have reminisced how Jesus explained to Martha that He was the Resurrection.

Jesus revealed Only to the Samaritan Woman that He was the Messiah.

Only Women would have recalled how Jesus said that unless you become like a child, you cannot enter the kingdom, and that Jesus referred to Himself as a Mother hen.

Probably the most embarrassing verses in the Bible for men are Matt 26:56,

"Then all the disciples ran away, forsaking Him."

"And leaving Him, all fled." Mark 14:50. One man even ran away naked!

Perhaps it was the servant-Girl who revealed all the humiliations and horrors of Jesus' trial, how He was questioned, mocked, spit on, whipped, beaten, given a royal robe and a crown of thorns. Perhaps it was Pilate's Wife.

<u>Surely, it was Jesus' Mother, Mary, who noticed the soldiers gambling for her Son's tunic, "And the tunic was seamless, woven from the top through all." (John 19:23)</u>

There are many details about the crucifixion which only a faithful person would have dared to reveal.

Actually, there are a few brave men who stand out among the rest. One is the centurion who admitted, "Truly this *One* was Son of GOD." (Matt 27:54)

Another was Joseph of Arimathea who asked for the body of Jesus and then laid Him in his own tomb.

Also, Nicodemus brought a hundred pounds of spices and helped Joseph wrap the body of Jesus for his burial.

No one knew about the Women buying spices and bringing them to the tomb just before dawn on the first of the week.

"And the sabbath passing, Mary Magdalene and Mary the m*other* of James and Salome, bought spices, so that coming they might anoint Him." (Mark 16:1)

Only Women reported about the great earthquake and described the angel of the Lord,

"And, behold! A great earthquake occurred! For descending from Heaven and coming near, an angel of *the* Lord rolled away the stone from the door and *was* sitting on it. And the appearance of him was as lightning and his clothing white as snow." (Mt 28:2,3)

<u>How would we know about the earthquake or the angel rolling away the huge stone unless the Women told us?</u>

The Women were shocked when they stumbled upon the guards, lifeless on the ground,

"And those keeping guard were shaken from the fear of him, and they became as dead *men*." (Matt 28:4)

<u>How would we know about the guards, being struck with terror, collapsed on the ground, unless the Women told us?</u>

My favorite painting, "*He Is Risen*," by Arthur Hughes 1832–1915. <u>The Women see the guards with their faces on the ground as if they are dead men.</u>

<u>Patriarchy had fallen!!</u>

The guards dropped as dead men when they saw the angel.

They were later bribed to lie, saying that they were asleep.

"GOD can, by one and the same means, comfort his servants, and terrify his enemies. The resurrection of Christ is a subject of terror to the servants of sin, and a subject of consolation to the sons of GOD; because it is a proof of the resurrection of both, the one to shame and everlasting contempt - the other to eternal glory and joy." – *Clarke*

The Women did not fall on the ground as dead Women. In fact, the angel of the Lord talked with them,

"He is not here, for He was raised, as He said. Come, see the place where the Lord was lying. And going quickly, say to His disciples that He was raised from the dead. And behold! He goes before you into Galilee. You will see Him there. Behold! I told you." (Matt 28:6,7)

The Women ran quickly, with fear and great joy, to report this to the disciples.

Three days earlier, the power of GOD knocked out the whole regiment of soldiers (500 - 1000 men, *Matthew Henry*).

"Therefore as He said to them, I AM, they went away into the rear and fell to the earth." (John 18:6) The power of His Name forced them all backwards.

* We can trace every word and footstep and emotion of the whole Resurrection morning, all because of the Women's information. *

Astoundingly, we even know some of the Women's names. It is written that Mary Magdalene and Joanna and Mary the Mother of James, and Salome and other Women were with them, on Resurrection morning.

The Women ran and told the disciples what they saw.

The men accused the Women of telling them nonsense, but the <u>Risen Lord scolded the men</u> for not believing the Women.

"And *He* reproached their unbelief and hardness of heart, because they did not believe those who had seen Him, having been raised." (Mark 16:14)

We would have nothing without the Women's testimonies.

<u>Women hurried and ran</u> to tell the good news. After the angel told Mary she would bear the Son of GOD,

"And rising up in these days, Mariam (*Mary*) went into the hill country with haste to a city of Judah." (Luke 1:39)

Elizabeth "cried out with a loud voice," the arrival of her "Lord."

Anna, an old Widow who never departed from the temple, instantly went out to the city to tell all those in Jerusalem "eagerly expecting redemption."

The Samaritan Woman "left her waterpot" and ran to tell the "men" in her city, about the Messiah.

On Resurrection morning, the angel of the Lord appeared to the Women,

"And going away from the tomb quickly, with fear and great joy, they ran to report to His disciples." (Matt 28:8)

Suddenly, Women had value after Jesus rose from the dead.

Before the Resurrection, Women were not allowed to speak to men and they could not be witnesses.

Afterward, without delay, Women were running all over the place, telling everyone, even men, about the Risen Lord.

After the Resurrection, Women's words were instantly highly esteemed. They had privileged information!

Women became vital in the community, sharing their personal experiences and passing down the cherished words of the Lord, <u>long before they were ever written</u>.

People were desperate to hear everything they could about Jesus. The Women were excited, evangelizing. <u>The men were still in hiding.</u>

"And Mariam (*Mary*) kept all these words, meditating in her heart." (Luke 2:19) Now, finally Mary could reveal the truths and people would listen.

The Women at the empty tomb --

"remembered His Words. And returning from the tomb, they reported all these things to the Eleven, and to all the rest." (Luke 24:8,9).

* Now, finally the Women were free to speak and the men would have to hear them. *

The birth of Christianity flourished because of Women's testimonies.

After the Resurrection, the Women were not afraid to speak or to be seen or to be heard.

Women became notable leaders and teachers, and people gathered in their homes.

Paul gave Women special greetings and he acknowledged their prominence among the believers.

Paul did not praise Women because of their good cooking or housekeeping.

These Women were Essential after the Resurrection.

After Peter got out of jail, he went directly to the house of Mary (Acts 12), where many were gathered together praying.

After Paul got out of jail, he went to Lydia's house (Acts 16).

Timothy's faith is the result of his Grandmother Lois and his Mother Eunice teaching him (2 Tim 1).

Behind these men were Exceptional Believing Women!

Those first years must have been just buzzing with Women circulating their experiences. The number of believers grew rapidly because of Women.

Women's voices became exceedingly important, especially after the Resurrection.

Acts tells us of several Women who had the first meetings in their homes and others who led prayer and worship services.

Paul gives credit to many Women who taught men. They preached and explained the scriptures to men!

These Women did not have subordinate roles. They were very active as prophets, deacons and outstanding among the apostles.

If Women had been silent, they would not have been persecuted.

Women were hunted down and thrown in prison the same as men.

<u>Women were martyrs the same as men.</u>

We have no idea how many Women gave their lives for this Gospel.

<u>Jesus never told Women to be silent, EVER.</u>

Men gave the command for the great stone to be sealed, <u>because of Fear.</u>

On Resurrection morning, the angel of the Lord rolled it back, and Jesus gave the command, His seal of approval, for Women to preach, <u>because of LOVE.</u>

"GO and TELL."

Jesus authorized and enabled Women to use their voice, especially after the Resurrection! Women are special, and Chosen to be part of the plan of Salvation.

GOD needs faithful men, Women and even children, to lead in spreading this good news, and to serve by showing love to a hurting world. The Gospels contain Jesus' words and actions, which entitle Women of today to use their talents to empower them to do what GOD calls them to do.

When Jesus Came

After long years of waiting for the prophecies to be fulfilled, suddenly Redemption was at hand! At last, GOD sent His Son, to set us free. From oppression to liberation. From bondage to blessings. From silence to shouts of praise!

The New Testament is a new era. Jesus came to heal the broken-hearted and to set free those who are oppressed.

<u>Our Gospels are bursting with Women who were compelled to proclaim the glad tidings, even before Jesus was born.</u>

<u>These Women are the forerunners of Christianity, breaking the patriarchal mold, framing the miraculous.</u>

Children were also inspired to give loud praises to the Lord.

Each of the following Women and children exalted a different aspect of our Lord's Deity.

They were all filled with the Holy Spirit, long before Pentecost. Only the Holy Spirit could have revealed what they knew.

Only by GOD's grace and with great faith could these Women and children express such courageous and glorious acts of love.

The Holy Spirit overshadowed Mary, the Mother of Jesus, and she was the first to give praise to her "Savior."

Upon seeing Mary, Elizabeth was filled with the Holy Spirit, and she was the first to cry out joyously with a loud voice for her "Lord."

After recognizing the long awaited Child, Anna the prophetess was the first to declare the "Redeemer" to the city of Jerusalem.

Jesus went out of His way to find a foreign Woman,

"And it was needful for Him to pass through Samaria." (John 4:4) He knew there was a Woman there, who yearned to worship in spirit and in truth. Jesus revealed Only to her that He was the "Messiah."

She was the first Gentile to preach the "Christ." The men had gone to buy food and they did not convert even one person, but the Samaritan Woman evangelized her entire city.

When Jesus called the children into the temple, they did not simply walk in unnoticed. They were moved to cry out, "Son of David."

After telling Jesus that she believed her brother will rise again on the last day, Jesus revealed Only to Martha, that He was the "Resurrection," and she reverenced Him as the "Christ, the Son of GOD."

Before Jesus was crucified, Mary of Bethany dared to be the first Woman to perform a religious function, which only men had claimed. She anointed Jesus, the "Anointed One." (John 12, Acts 4:26,27)

On Resurrection morning, Jesus appeared to the Women Only and He told them,

"Do not fear. Go tell your brothers that they may go into Galilee, and there they will see Me." (Matt 28:10).

How wonderful that the Risen Lord comforted the Women, again telling them not to have fear.

In the garden she was weeping, mourning for the One she loved. Mary Magdalene was the one GOD Chose to announce the

"Risen Lord." (John 20:18)

"Mary Magdalene comes reporting to the disciples that she had seen the Lord, and that He said to her these things."

The Holy Spirit kept working through Women after the Resurrection.

They were teachers and prophets and maids. They held prayer services and meetings in their homes, and they made clothing for the poor.

These Women were being hunted, yet they rejoiced and proclaimed the Risen Lord.

Priscilla and Aquila had to leave Rome. Lydia and other Women worshiped GOD outside of their town by the river. The Lord had opened their hearts. Lydia was the first convert in Europe.

GOD even used a slave Girl who was possessed, because her heart was right. For days she was driven to follow Paul, crying out, "These men are slaves of the <u>Most High GOD</u>, who proclaim to us a way of <u>salvation</u>!" (Acts 16:17)

Old and young, Gentile and Jew,

slave and free,

before most men even knew what was

going on, GOD revealed to these Women

and children the most precious news of all -

*** <u>Salvation had arrived!!!</u> ***

Indeed, Jesus was like no other man. It became immediately clear that Jesus treated Women with justice and mercy.

Jesus was very concerned about Women's spiritual and financial needs, even their sexual rights.

Jesus didn't ignore Women, He taught them, and He made sure to bless their children.

Jesus acknowledged Women, He defended them, and then He summoned them to speak.

Jesus taught in new and revolutionary ways, mostly outdoors and in people's homes. He welcomed all who would listen: the blind, the lame, even lepers.

Jesus included Women in the family of GOD, calling them Daughters. He healed them and their children, Gentiles, too.

Jesus touched Women, even bleeding Women, even a dead Girl. Jesus let Women and children touch Him, too.

No longer are Women unclean!

In most cases Women were terrified to be noticed in public, yet Jesus called them out, against all cultural traditions, against religious rules, against the minds of men, even against their own wishes.

Generally, the Women followed in the background and listened to Jesus.

The most common sound you hear from Women in the Gospels is their <u>weeping</u>.

Most Women tried to remain quite invisible in the Gospels, as was expected, but some had great faith and courage to go beyond their given boundaries.

One Woman crawled through the crowds to touch the hem of His garment, but trembled with fear when Jesus asked her to identify herself.

Another Woman had a conversation with Jesus at a well, but she ran away when the men arrived.

One Woman dared to sit at His feet, but she was quiet. Later she anointed Jesus before He was crucified, but she never spoke then either.

The men were indignant (Matt 26, Mark 14, Luke 7, John 12). She only wiped her tears off of His feet with her hair.

Never before did a man give a Woman priority over a religious man.

Woman never entered the men's inner court of the temple.

Jesus gave radical new teachings on marriage and divorce, warning men not to even look at a Woman with lust.

Jesus laid hands on sick Women and answered their deepest concerns.

No longer are Women inferior!

Never before did a man stop to bless children and to heal blind beggars.

It's a wonder that Jesus even saw the bent Woman.

Jesus was teaching in the temple, but He stopped and called her. She had to climb up all those stairs and enter the forbidden men's area. Then Jesus laid hands on her, healed her and called her "daughter."

The priests were very angry. I wonder what they were more disturbed about, that it was a Sabbath, or that a Woman was in their territory?

Never before did a man pay such attention to Widows, or encourage Women to learn the spiritual life.

It was unheard of, for Women to be told not to cook so much. Martha was "distracted about much serving." Jesus saw that she was "anxious and troubled about many things."

*Maryanne Rempel wonders,

"When is our day of rest?"*

Jesus taught men, Women and children, even Gentiles. He insisted that Women be treated equally and with respect.

Jesus really emphasized that men need to take care of Women.

One Woman was living with a man and He didn't judge her.

Jesus saved a Woman's life, even though she was caught in adultery.

Another Woman was called "sinful" by men, but He welcomed her anointing and her love.

No more shame and blame for Women's sexuality.

Jesus never saw Women as sinful!

Never before did a man use children to teach important lessons.

After Jesus drove out the money changers, the blind and the lame came to Him in the temple, and He healed them.

Jesus must have called them because they, too, were labeled unclean. Then the children cried out in the temple, "Hosanna to the Son of David."

Again, the chief priests and scribes were furious. Why were they so upset? Because Women were in the temple also! (Matt 21:14 - 16) Where there are "babes and sucklings" … there are Mothers!

Suddenly, Women are equal!!

Jesus taught Women, blessed Women, healed Women, appreciated and honored Women.

Jesus absolutely wanted Women to proclaim His message on Resurrection morning.

** What is really shocking is how Jesus treated the men. **

You will notice that in every encounter where there was an interaction with Women or children, whether it was outside, in the temple or even if a Woman came into the same room, the men became severely agitated, even enraged.

Jesus refused to chase the Women and children away.

He got angry and called the men names, pointed out their wicked traditions, exposing their motives and sins.

He was never harsh with Women, though.

There is not one incident where Jesus neglected or put down a Woman or a child.

He always treated them with dignity and respect.

There is something quite reversed in the New Testament.

The roles were turned upside down. The men were silenced and the Women were prompted to speak.

At the beginning of the Gospels, the Women are scared and in hiding. At the end, the men are scared and in hiding. The teachings are in favor of Women's protection and the reprimands are given to the men (do not lust after Women, leave her alone).

Women are called Daughters. Men are called hypocrites.

** On almost every page, Jesus praises the Women for their great faith. He then chastises the men for their unbelief, and for the way they treated Women. **

It is surprising that the writers included so many of these contrasts.

In comparison to the Women, the Gospels are actually quite humiliating for the men, from Zacharias to Peter.

Considering the culture and the pride of men and the challenging aspect of every Woman's memoir, the scribes must have also had radical faith and tenacity to stand behind these records.

We know that some of the early writers were persecuted to death for their loyalty and honesty.

We must recognize the sacrifice of those early transcribers and honor them.

Contrary to what Women have been taught about being silent, you will now discover that Jesus all but <u>forced Women to speak</u>.

You will be amazed when you read how often Jesus invited and challenged Women to come forward, in the middle of the crowd, up into the temple, and when He rose again.

The Woman with a bent back (Luke 13), "walks up the aisle to the platform with trembling feet, and stands in a most unusual position, out in public, among all the men! Gently He spoke to her and "laid His hands on her," and behold! not only is she "loosed from her infirmity" of a bowed back, but also of a silenced tongue; "she was made straight and glorified GOD." –

Bushnell, Katharine. GOD's Word to Women (Annotated) (Kindle Locations 6632-6635). Crowning Educational. Kindle Edition.

It is quite interesting to see how the Women develop their voices.

They praise. They whisper. They evangelize their whole city. They shout. They speak quietly. They ask boldly. They mourn. They wail. Then they proclaim.

The Women had profound faith and followed Jesus for three years.

During those days, Jesus prepared them for that glorious moment, when He appeared to <u>Women Only</u>.

Then He instructed them to

"GO and TELL."

It had to be that way, to defeat patriarchy.

Jesus showed the utmost love and respect for Women and children. Women have always been part of GOD's plan and are still urgently needed for the kingdom.

Women will always have a valuable role in spreading the Gospel, standing up for what is right, overcoming fears and cultural restraints.

Jesus even brought Women and children into the forbidden men's area of the temple.

When Jesus breathed His last, the huge veil which concealed the tabernacle in the Holy of Holies was torn in two pieces, from top to bottom.

Patriarchy was defeated!!!

No Women = No Christianity

Jesus made Women come out of hiding, and He enticed them to speak. One can almost feel the sorrows and the joys of these Women. They have so much pain and passion and extreme faith.

Right from the opening chapters, it's <u>All about the Women. Women are absolutely the founders of Christianity.</u>

Without Mary's faith and cooperation we would have <u>No Child</u>!

<u>"Where did your Christ come from?</u>

<u>From GOD and a Woman!</u>

<u>Man had nothing to do with Him."</u>

- Sojourner Truth, *Ain't I a Woman?* Speech delivered in 1851 at Women's Convention, Akron, Ohio. Without the Women's deep devotion we would not know much of what happened at the cross!

<u>Christianity hinges on the faith and the words of a few Women.</u>

Imagine for a moment if the Women had not come to the tomb…

Without the Women's faithful presence on that Resurrection morning we would have <u>no Christianity</u>!

Realistically, if Women had not <u>told and retold and retold</u> their experiences, we would have <u>No Gospels</u>.

<u>The men all ran away.</u>

They were <u>all afraid.</u>

The men <u>went into hiding.</u>

The men would have never thought about going to look for the tomb.

After Jesus was arrested, <u>the men all ran away</u>.

The men were <u>still hiding on the third day.</u>

The <u>Women followed</u> Jesus as He was led to His crucifixion.

The <u>Women wailed</u> in the streets.

The <u>Women stayed</u> at the cross.

The <u>Women went to the tomb</u> and took note of the body, how Jesus was laid.

The <u>Women bought and prepared spices</u> to anoint Him.

The <u>Women went to the tomb</u> early that morning...

Even if the men had thought of it, they did not know where to go. They did not know where Jesus was laid.

Peter had to follow Mary Magdalene back to the empty tomb.

Try to imagine the Gospels without any of the Women's words or details or actions. It is not possible.

** The Conception and the Resurrection are the two miraculous moments which overturned the history of the world, and GOD relied on Women to make it happen and to make it known. **

Compared to all the other religions, you might say that this is a <u>Woman's religion</u>.

Christianity is based completely on Two Miracles, where <u>GOD Deliberately Chose Women Only</u>.

Without the Conception and Resurrection of Jesus, we Could Not have Christianity.

*** <u>Christianity is founded totally on the Conception and Resurrection of Jesus Christ.</u> ***

<u>It's the Women who make us know the birth and death and Resurrection of Jesus.</u>

A Woman at the beginning and Women at the end. Mary says "Yes!"

Mary Magdalene announces that she has "seen the Lord."

The Angel Gabriel appeared to Mary.

The Risen Lord appeared to Mary Magdalene.

Mary was highly favored by GOD to be the Mother of Jesus.

Mary Magdalene was favored by Jesus to "GO and TELL."

Both Women were reassured not to be afraid.

Without hesitation, Mary "rising up" went "with haste." (Luke 1:39).

Mary Magdalene and the other Mary left "the tomb quickly, with fear and great joy, they ran to report to His disciples."

The Women were thrilled to cooperate with GOD's plan. Mary's spirit "exulted in GOD my Savior." (Luke 1:47).

Mary Magdalene "ran" "quickly with fear and great joy."

For centuries, Mary Magdalene has been maligned, discredited, and painted with a filthy brush, but she deserves the highest recognition, together with Mary the Mother of Jesus.

Early Christianity has repeatedly acknowledged Mary Magdalene as the 'Apostle to the Apostles' yet her witness and testimony of the Risen Lord are pushed out of Easter readings, with the focus being on Peter, who never even got to see Him!!

"Women In Ancient Christianity: The New Discoveries" "Scholar Karen King examines the evidence concerning women's important place in early Christianity. Mary Magdalene was indeed an influential figure, but as a prominent disciple and leader of one wing of the early Christian movement that promoted women's leadership."

Is Mary Magdalene not the most important source of information, about the Resurrection? Without her testimony, we would not know about that most solemn, glorious morning.

We would not have Salvation! Christianity depends entirely on the faith and words of Women.

**** <u>Mary was Chosen to be the Mother of our Lord – the Most Precious Moment in History.</u> ****

**** <u>Mary Magdalene was Chosen to tell the world about the Risen Lord – the Second Most Precious Moment in History.</u> ****

We cannot have one without the other.

* Both of these Women hold the most Valuable Keys to Christianity. *

We cannot imagine the sacrifice those Women made, to co-operate with GOD's plan of Salvation.

Archeology tells us Mary Magdalene was a fundamental leader in the early community of believers and a great teacher, but we do not realize the grave danger she was in, for her knowledge and experience of the Resurrection.

<u>If Jesus Chose to reveal Himself first and foremost to Mary Magdalene, should we not honor her as much?</u>

Women appear to be quiet in the background at the beginning, but they do all the praising and evangelizing.

They are the faithful ones. They follow. They support. They listen. They anoint. They are in nerve-racking situations. They give their lives.

They say "YES" and then they …

"GO and TELL."

What did Jesus do for Women?

Your hearts will melt when you read how much Jesus included Women in His ministry, and after He rose again.

Jesus spoke with authority, allowing Women to learn alongside the men, performing miracles on Women no matter what day it was, and sending the crowds away so He could bring a young Girl back to life.

Despite men's thoughts and attitudes of wanting to send Women away, Jesus accepted Women for their extraordinary acts of love.

Jesus welcomed and approved of being anointed by a Woman and He exalted her, commanding us to remember her Forever.

Suddenly Women can anoint!

You will be astounded at how frequently Jesus got angry with the men, on account of Women. He spoke sternly against abuse and poverty.

Jesus caused society to recognize the need to take care of their Women and children, especially Widows.

Mostly, He scolded the religious leaders and law-makers because they oppress the poor.

Jesus' words are crucial and life giving for Women, helping them to believe that they Deserve to be Loved and Supported.

He made Women realize that they have a right to be heard and Protected.

Jesus went out of His way for Women. He noticed them and spoke up for them. He called them amidst the crowds, in front of men in the temple, in homes, alone at a well, or caught in a trap.

Not only did Jesus give Women respect, He elevated them by making public displays of how they should be treated equally, and with dignity.

No longer could men simply send away their Wives without giving them half the matrimonial property, no matter what the excuse. If the men did not want to give the Women a divorce, Jesus blamed the men for the Women's adultery.

Jesus inverted all the traditions of men concerning Women's sexuality. He declared that Women can even leave their husbands. What liberation!

Jesus was an exceptional defender of Women's rights. We just don't realize all that He did.

Women will find out that Jesus is their teacher, healer and outstanding protector. Jesus enjoyed listening to Women, blessing them and teaching them. He encouraged Women, informed them of their rights, and of their valuable place in the kingdom.

The status of Women and children was lifted to be equal with men. Jesus was concerned about Women's work, and moved by their tears.

Now Women know that they have the right to name their children. No longer are Women bound and limited by society's roles and expectations.

No longer are Women to be Abused.

Jesus made Women visible. Until Jesus came, Women were invisible. He encouraged them to learn and to speak in public. Jesus appointed Women to be His witnesses and heralds of His Resurrection.

These Women are real. They are our spiritual Mothers, our heritage. No longer are Women defined by their sexuality.

Jesus opened the doors to Women's education, their purpose and destiny.

Women will realize just how invaluable they were in the entire life of Christ, from His Conception to His Resurrection, and especially afterward.

In His crowning triumph, Jesus awarded Women with the highest honor, giving them the Royal Commission.

Jesus favored Women to be His privileged witnesses.

Women were selected to "GO and TELL" about the most glorious, miraculous event ever!!!

** GOD Chose Only Women! **

On Resurrection morning, the Women came while it was still dark. They "ran" to tell the men that someone had taken the body of the Lord.

Peter ran, too, but the Women Ran First. When Peter got to the tomb, he saw the linens, but that's all.

Peter left.

The Women stayed.

The Risen Lord never appeared to Peter. John 20:10

Peter walked away confused and was left in the dust.

After Peter left, Mary Magdalene stayed at the empty tomb, grieving for the One she loved.

Two angels appeared to Mary Magdalene, and asked her why she was weeping.

Suddenly, the Risen Lord appeared to her and also asked her why she was weeping.

Jesus called her by name, "Mary." Then He instructed her, "But go to My brothers and say to them…" (John 20:15 - 17)

*** Jesus Deliberately Wanted ONLY Women To See Him. ***

Even the guards did not get to see anything. Jesus did not let any man see Him.

"And the *ones* keeping guard were shaken from the fear of him (an angel of *the* Lord), and they became as dead *men*." (Matthew 28:4)

They had fallen as dead men on the ground.

The guards woke up confused and were literally left in the dust.

* The angels appeared, spoke,

<u>Only to the Women</u> *

* Mt 28:5, Mark 16:5, Luke 24:4, Jn 20:13 *

* Jesus appeared, and spoke,

<u>Only to the Women</u> *

* Matt 28:9, Mark 16:9, John 20:16 *

Mary Magdalene reported, "she had seen the Lord." (John 20:18)

Peter came looking for a dead body, but he found only the burial cloths.

The guards were hired to watch a dead body, but they became as dead men.

The guards were right outside the sealed tomb. Peter walked right into the empty tomb. The men were all confused and they all left.

Peter wondered what happened to the body. The guards wondered how they would explain 'no body.'

Peter walked away and got back to his friends. The guards walked away to the chief priests and got silver.

<u> The Risen Lord never appeared to any man in Jerusalem. </u>

Mary Magdalene arrived before daylight. She stayed behind after Peter left, alone in the garden, crying at the empty tomb.

My favourite song is *"In The Garden"* written by C. Austin Miles, March 1912.

When Jesus revealed Himself, calling her by name, she instantly knew it was the Risen Lord, and was filled with ecstasy and excitement.

She ran and broadcast to the men and Peter that she had found the living, glorified body of her Lord!

Mary Magdalene exploded with passion and joy and jubilation! She had <u>seen and heard and talked with her Risen Lord</u>!

This was GOD's precise plan.

We must never forget that GOD Chose Women, "GO and TELL."

Mary is given and will always have the Highest Honor, being selected to be the Mother of Our Lord.

The Women who see the Risen Lord are given the Second Highest Honor ever bestowed on Women.

They are the privileged witnesses of His Resurrection.

Women were Chosen to be the Only Proclaimers of that Glorious Resurrection Day.

Jesus Deliberately Chose Only Women To See Him!!

* The Resurrection was Reserved for Women Only!! *

THE RESURRECTION - RESERVED FOR WOMEN!

Organized religion has long suppressed the fact that Jesus appeared Only to Mary Magdalene and the other Women at the empty tomb.

*** The overlooked point is that Jesus could just as easily have appeared to Peter when he arrived at the tomb, but Clearly and Deliberately He did not! ***

Twice it is recorded, at the last supper, Jesus told the men they would have to go to Galilee in order to see Him.

"But after My resurrection I will go before you into Galilee." (Matt 26:32)

"But after the raising up of Me, I will go before you into Galilee." (Mark 14:28)

On Resurrection morning, the Women were specifically instructed by the angel, to go tell his disciples and Peter, to go over "there" to Galilee.

"And going quickly say to His disciples that He was raised from the dead. And behold! He goes before you into Galilee. You will see Him there. Behold! I told you." (Matt 28:7)

"But go, say to the disciples and to Peter, He goes before you into Galilee. You will see Him there, even as He told you." (Mark 16:7)

The angel confirms what Jesus had said, that the men must go "there," to "Galilee" in order to see Him.

At first the angel told the Women to go tell the disciples and Peter to go to Galilee. Then Jesus appeared to the Women Himself.

"Then Jesus said to them, Do not fear. Go tell your brothers that they may go into Galilee, and there they will see Me." (Matt 28:10)

That makes FIVE different verses which say the exact same thing.

FIVE times it says the word Galilee.

THREE of those verses are from Jesus Himself.

TWO are from the angel at the empty tomb. Every verse confirms that the disciples and Peter had to go all the way "there" to "Galilee" in order to see the Risen Lord.

"Galilee" Matt 26:32 (Jesus),

"Galilee" Mark 14:28 (Jesus),

"Galilee" Matt 28:7 (Angel),

"Galilee" Mark 16:7 (Angel),

"Galilee" Matt 28:10 (Jesus).

"there" Matt 28:7 (Angel),

"there" Mark 16:7 (Angel),

"there" Matt 28:10 (Jesus)

What we have not heard is that, from Jerusalem to <u>Galilee</u>, it is approximately 193 km (120 miles), very rocky and mountainous terrain!

On foot, this would have been a long journey to get "<u>there</u>."

A tourism site from Israel, says it is 131 km (81 miles) between Jerusalem and Nazareth in <u>Galilee</u>. Google maps says there are two routes to Nazareth, one is 153 km, the other 160 km (100 miles).

The disciples were told to meet on a mountain in <u>Galilee</u>, so these distances will vary.

Why so far?

Why didn't Jesus just appear to the men when they were at the tomb?

The men only saw Jesus, after they got over "<u>there</u>," in <u>Galilee</u>.

* <u>The men had to walk at least 100 miles to see Him!!</u> *

Perhaps Jesus appeared to those two men walking to Emmaus on the "same" day (Luke 24:13) because the eleven needed to hear that Jesus was alive from male witnesses. "And they having heard that He lives, and was seen by her, they did not believe." (Mark 16:11).

> How humiliating for the men to be told about the Resurrection by Women.

It was obvious that the men had not believed the Women as they were still in Jerusalem late that "same" night. "And, behold, two of them were going on the same day to a village being sixty stadia distant from Jerusalem, which was named Emmaus." (Luke 24:13)

After Jesus revealed Himself, (Luke 24:33,34) "And rising up in the same hour, they went back to Jerusalem, and found, having been gathered together, the Eleven, and those with them, saying, The Lord really was raised and appeared to Simon."

This reveals their shock and dismay that the Women had actually told the truth.

** Still Jesus did not appear to men in Jerusalem. It was seven miles out. **

Although Jesus appeared to the eleven in Matt 28:16, "But the eleven disciples went into <u>Galilee</u>, to the mount where Jesus appointed them." *The JFB Commentary* states, "but certainly not before the second week after the resurrection, and probably somewhat later."

The People's New Testament Commentary on Matthew 28:16 confirms, "It was on the second Sunday after the resurrection; the second Lord's day in the history of the world."

Wesley's Commentary says, "On the next Sunday."

Robertson's Word Pictures Commentary says, "That is the next Sunday evening, on the eighth day."

Also, here is a title - § 179. THE APPEARANCE TO THE DISCIPLES THE NEXT SUNDAY NIGHT… - *ROBERTSON, A.T.: A Harmony of the Gospels for Students of the Life of Christ* (illustrated) (Kindle Locations 7281-7282).

There are quite a few other commentaries which confirm these, but I thought five was sufficient.

** We know that the men had to go to "Galilee" first, to see the Risen Lord. (approximately 100 miles) **

It is recorded in Five verses that He "goes before you into Galilee." (Matt 26:32, 28:7,10, Mark 14:28, 16:7)

In John 20:19, it says Jesus appeared to them, "Then it being evening on that day, the first of the sabbaths," but it was likely the following week. It says "that day," not the "same day."

The men and Peter could not be in two places, 100 miles apart, at the same hour. They were still in Jerusalem the "same day" when the two men from Emmaus came back and told them.

** How long does it take for eleven men to pack their donkeys, and then walk 100 miles? **

We will never know all the reasons why <u>GOD Chose Only Women</u> to tell the greatest information ever heard.

<u>The evidence is rock solid, in all four Gospels</u>.

*** <u>The Resurrection of Jesus Christ is the pivotal moment in the entire history of the world and GOD relied on Women Only to "GO and TELL."</u> ***

*** <u>Jesus definitely commissioned Women Only.</u> ***

"Mary Magdalene comes reporting to the disciples that she had seen the Lord, and that He said to her these things." (John 20:18)

Jesus reserved the Most Magnificent Hour for Women.

He specifically wanted Only Women to proclaim His Resurrection.

It was totally on purpose!!

Jesus demolished every barrier Women had to face.

"There cannot be Jew nor Greek, there is no slave nor freeman, there is no male and female; for you are all one in Christ Jesus." (Gal 3:28)

The thick veil was torn in two, so Women can enter boldly.

Patriarchy was defeated!!!

Besides respecting the Women publicly and treating them equally, the most transforming gift Jesus gave Women was…

Jesus gave Women a voice!

* Women were selected to broadcast His Resurrection. *

Women who were timid and shy and meek and humble and scared, who were forbidden to talk to men, who were so restricted, were suddenly assigned to proclaim this glorious news, to reveal this earth-shattering love of GOD. *

* A Woman proclaims at the beginning (Mary's Magnificat) and Women proclaim at the end (Risen Lord)! *

The Resurrection message was a privilege reserved for Women. The entire history of the world culminated in that one supreme, sovereign morning.

It was GOD's finest hour. That holy hour was the zenith of Jesus' life and He gave Women the unrivalled honor to

"GO and TELL."

Women shattered the silence!!!

Women were instructed to proclaim that Jesus Rose from the Dead.

Jesus became Visible to the Women Only --

The Women saw Him.

The Women heard Him.

The Women spoke with Him.

** Jesus could have revealed Himself to the men, but He authorized Women Only. **

What an imperial honor!!

In Jerusalem, at the empty tomb, Jesus did not appear when the men arrived.

On Resurrection morning, GOD selected Women, Only Women, and gave them the most priceless message this world has ever heard.

Women had to tell the men.

The Women were delegated by GOD to announce the most life-altering news ever!

Mary Magdalene proclaimed the very first Resurrection message!

JESUS IS ALIVE!!!!!

Jesus Never restricted Women in any way. He completely gave Women the honor to lead men into the new era.

Women were appointed to be the ones to declare the most excellent message.

Peter was there too, After the Women showed him where the tomb was, but Jesus never appeared to him.

Peter had to walk 100 miles.

Women were destined to be preachers by Jesus Himself!

<u>The Resurrection of Jesus Christ marks the most significant breaking news the world has ever known.</u>

<u>Jesus Rose from the dead!!</u>

<u>There has never been a more colossal victory.</u>

<u>No other achievement is comparable.</u>

Every detail about this triumphant occasion was planned and prophesied from before the beginning of time.

<u>We cannot fully grasp the Resurrection without thinking of the Women who were there.</u>

<u>All four Gospels recount specific information about that exceptional morning, which Only the Women would have known about.</u>

There are many details describing Jesus' Resurrection, all pointing to the credibility of those who were there, all of whom were Women.

One clear message is that <u>Jesus designated Women to be proclaimers of this mind-blowing Miracle of Miracles.</u>

Everything we know about the Resurrection is what we see through the <u>eyes</u> of Mary Magdalene and the other Women.

Every word we read about the Resurrection came through the <u>voice</u> of Mary Magdalene and the other Women.

Jesus told the Women to "GO and TELL,"

NOT to be Silent. EVER**

ADAM -- Life changing bible study

"Adam was not deceived," 1 Timothy 2:14

"In Adam all die," 1 Corinthians 15:22

"By one man [person] sin entered into the world," Romans 5:12

"Through the offense of one many be dead," Romans 5:15

"it was by one that sinned," Romans 5:16

"The judgment was by one to condemnation," Romans 5:16

"By one man's offense death reigned,"

    [death reigned] "by one," Romans 5:17

"By the offense of one judgment came upon all men to condemnation," Romans 5:18

"By one man's disobedience" Romans 5:19

"Death reigned from Adam to Moses, even over them that had not sinned after the similitude of Adam's transgression, who is the figure of Him that was to come" Romans 5:14

"After the fourth chapter of Genesis, Eve is never referred to again in the O. T. …But when we come to the N. T., there is a striking contrast between the estimate put upon Adam's and Eve's conduct. …Of Adam it is plainly said that his conduct brought sin into the world. …the *disobedience of Adam*, this was what brought universal destruction."

"The greater culpability of Eve as causing the fall is *taught by tradition only*." -- Katharine Bushnell.

EVE

"The woman being [thoroughly] deceived was [literally, "became"] in the transgression." Weymouth renders this, more accurately, "was thoroughly deceived, and so became involved"   1 Timothy 2:14

"the serpent beguiled [literally, "thoroughly deceived"] Eve through his subtlety."   2 Corinthians 11:3

Both these passages employ the same verb in the Greek original, "to deceive," with a prefix meaning "thoroughly." The verb itself is the same one which is used of Adam in our first quotation regarding him excepting that in Adam's case there is no prefix, as in Eve's case.

We give the sole references to Eve in the Bible, after the Genesis story. Nor is Eve even remotely referred to elsewhere in the Bible.

Eight times over, Paul declares "one person" alone was accountable for the Fall, and twice mentions that person as "Adam."

From *God's Word to Women,* by Katharine Bushnell, published by God's Word to Women, Inc, 2004. Entire article used with permission and gratitude. – (1923 edition)

Hebert, Adele. Jesus Loves Women So Much: All the Women and Children in the Gospels (Kindle Locations 3451-3452). Kindle Edition.

Secrets of the Cocoon

Whenever we see movies or paintings about Jesus and His Resurrection, we see a lovely draped cloth hanging over the edge of the stone slab where His body was laid.

Just think about this. When we have a cut on our finger, we put a band aid on it. After 3 days when we take it off, how does it look? It's in the <u>exact shape</u> of our finger, right? When blood dries, it remains in the same shape as it dried, on a cloth or band aid. Sometimes it is even stuck to our finger. It is definitely not flat or soft or pretty.

The custom of the Jews was to wind up the dead person in strips of linen cloths, which look like bandages.

These narrow strips were rolled around His body many times, and mixed with spices, <u>myrrh</u> and aloes. Nicodemus brought the spices.

The linen strips and myrrh were applied to Jesus' body. When the thick resin of the myrrh is exposed to the air, it dries quickly.

Finally, Jesus was covered with a fine linen shroud which Joseph of Arimathea purchased.

The Women were there and saw how Jesus' body was laid and wrapped.

Luk 23:55 And the women also, which came with him from Galilee, followed after, and beheld the sepulchre, and how his body was laid.

Mat_27:59 And when Joseph had taken the body, he wrapped it in a clean linen cloth,

Joh 19:39 And there came also Nicodemus, which at the first came to Jesus by night, and brought a mixture of myrrh and aloes, about an hundred pound *weight.*

Joh_19:40 Then took they the body of Jesus, and wound it in linen clothes with the spices, as the manner of the Jews is to bury.

On Resurrection morning, Mary Magdalene came to the tomb with the other Women.

What did the Women see?

Mat 28:2 And, behold, there was a great earthquake: for the angel of the Lord descended from heaven, and came and rolled back the stone from the door, and sat upon it.

Mat 28:3 His countenance was like lightning, and his raiment white as snow:

Mat 28:4 And for fear of him the keepers did shake, and became as dead *men.*

How else would we know all these great things if the Women had not told us?

Mat 28:5 And the angel answered and said unto the women, Fear not ye: for I know that ye seek Jesus, which was crucified.

Mat 28:6 He is not here: for he is risen, as he said. Come, see the place where the Lord lay.

What did the Women see?

The Women <u>saw</u> the angel, bright as lightening.

The Women <u>saw</u> the guards as dead men on the ground.

The Women <u>saw</u> the stone rolled away, with the angel sitting on it.

The <u>angel of the Lord invited</u> the Women to go inside the tomb.

The Women were the <u>First</u> to see the empty tomb.

The Women were <u>First</u> to see the fine linen shroud.

The Women were the <u>First</u> to see the stiff dried strips which wrapped his body.

The Women were <u>First</u> to see the empty shell, which was hard and molded to Jesus' body.

<u>How else would we know all these great things if the Women had not told us?</u>

"John Chrysostom, in the fourth century A.D., commented that "the myrrh used was a drug which adheres so closely to the body that the grave clothes could not easily be removed.""

The strips of cloth that wrapped Jesus' body were covered in dried blood and would have been stuck to Him.

These linen strips were also glued together, all in one piece because of the myrrh mixed with the dried blood.

After three days, it was hardened to the shape of His body.

Then the Women were told to "Go and Tell" the men that Jesus was raised and that they had to go to Galilee in order to see Him there.

Joh_20:6 Then cometh Simon Peter following him, and went into the sepulchre, and seeth the linen clothes lie,

Joh_20:7 And the napkin, that was about his head, not lying with the linen clothes, but wrapped together in a place by itself. (KJV)

The NECK HOLE!

The Only place that was not covered with the blood soaked linen and myrrh was –

the NECK HOLE!

The hardened cloth became a COCOON!

How could Jesus come out from that small hole?

Only by the miraculous power of the RESURRECTION!!

No wonder Peter left confused. He saw a hollow shell!

The folded cloth was the cloth which covered Jesus' head and face. It was folded and placed on the side which meant "it was finished."

The RESURRECTION happened exacted as predicted.

How Did Jesus Answer?

I never got trained in worldly ways to DEFEND myself.

I am usually way too honest and give answers to people who don't deserve to know anything about me. Then I kick myself for days afterward.

I needed help because certain people were always asking me personal questions and I didn't want to answer them anymore.

One day I decided Women need to learn how to answer because we are very naïve, usually an open book.

There are all kinds of people out there, mostly the insincere kind:

People who are nosey.

People who are jealous.

People who want to trap you with your information.

People who don't have a life.

People who don't respect your privacy.

People who make you exhausted with all their questions!!

>We need boundaries…..

When you are asked a question, the first thought that should come to your mind is,

>"Why are they asking me that?"

>**** I needed answers and Jesus is the answer to everything. ****

As I was reading the Gospels, I noticed that there were two kinds of people -- sincere and Not sincere.

There were also two kinds of answers that Jesus gave.

For those who were sincere, Jesus answered in very clear and simple ways, to teach them and to help them understand.

For those who were Not sincere, like those who were trying to trap Him, He answered their <u>Questions with a Question</u>.

Jesus did not give them an answer at all.

He also turned around and walked away many times. This would take some practise; we all want to be so nice.

I am still caught off guard when asked seemingly innocent questions.

Ask a friend to role play with you. Repeat several responses like,

"Why do you ask?"

"I don't discuss personal matters."

Be ready for those you have trouble with.

When asked something that bothered you, go home and ask yourself how you could answer them next time.

You will get better with time.

People who don't know you personally have no right to ask personal questions.

Read your Gospels.

Jesus is the answer to everything.

Made in the USA
Middletown, DE
23 June 2019